Marine Life

by Mary Miller

Editorial Offices: Glenview, Illinois • Parsippany, New Jersey • New York, New York
Sales Offices: Needham, Massachusetts • Duluth, Georgia • Glenview, Illinois
Coppell, Texas • Ontario, California • Mesa, Arizona

Every effort has been made to secure permission and provide appropriate credit for photographic material. The publisher deeply regrets any omission and pledges to correct errors called to its attention in subsequent editions.

Unless otherwise acknowledged, all photographs are the property of Scott Foresman, a division of Pearson Education.

Photo locators denoted as follows: Top (T), Center (C), Bottom (B), Left (L), Right (R), Background (Bkgd)

Opener ©Stuart Westmorland/Corbis; 1 ©Stuart Westmorland/Corbis; 3 ©Warren Morgan/Corbis; 5 ©Kennan Ward/Corbis; 6 (TR) ©Peter Steiner/Corbis, 6 ©Stuart Westmorland/Corbis; 7 © M. Harvey/Animals Animals/Earth Scenes; 9 ©David Muench/ Corbis; 10 ©Stuart Westmorland/Corbis; 11 (T) ©Raymond Gehman/Corbis, 11 (Inset) ©Brandon D. Cole/Corbis; 13 ©Scott T. Smith/Corbis; 14 ©Jeffrey L. Rotman/Corbis; 15 ©Anthony Redpath/Corbis; 16 ©Lawson Wood/Corbis; 18 ©Stuart Westmorland/ Corbis; 19 (B) ©Theo Allofs/Corbis, 19 (Inset) ©Ron Watts/Corbis; 20 (B) ©Stephen Frink/Corbis, 20 (Inset) ©Stuart Westmorland/Corbis; 21 ©Royalty-Free/Corbis, 21 (Inset) ©Stephen Frink/Corbis, 21 (Inset) ©Amos Nachoum/Corbis; 22 (Inset) ©Lawson Wood/ Corbis, 22 (B) Getty Images; 23 ©Stephen Frink/Corbis

ISBN: 0-328-13577-1

4 5 6 7 8 9 10 V0G1 14 13 12 11 10 09 08 07 06

An Ocean Home

More than seventy percent of Earth is covered by water. Most of it is in the Earth's oceans. Earth has four oceans: the Atlantic Ocean, the Pacific Ocean, the Indian Ocean, and the Arctic Ocean. These oceans meet the land along rocky coastlines, sandy beaches, salt marshes, and mud flats. People enjoy many activities along these coasts. Children play on sandy beaches. People hike along rocky coastlines. Birdwatchers visit salt marshes to look for migrating seabirds.

Because most of the living things you see every day are on land, you might think that life stops at the ocean shore. However, these coastlines and the ocean waters near them are homes to thousands of life forms.

Rocky Coast and Sandy Shore

Ocean coasts are difficult places to live near. Waves can be large and powerful. Also, because of tides, the water actually leaves the shore twice a day. A tide is the cycle of rising and lowering water that happens along ocean shores. When the tide goes out, many ocean animals are left high and dry.

Creatures that live along shorelines have developed ways of surviving waves and tides. Many creatures simply bury themselves in the sand or find a safe place to hide among the rocks.

Barnacles make a substance that "glues" them in place. This keeps them from being swept away by the tide. As the tide comes in and goes out, it carries small plants and animals that the barnacle catches and eats.

Mussels create tough, sticky threads, called byssal threads, to keep themselves in place. A mussel clings to rocks with about eighty byssal threads in the winter and thirty threads in the summer. When the tide goes out, mussels close up tight so that they won't dry out.

Mussels and starfish cling to a rock exposed at low tide.

Snails also live along the coastline. Snails have soft bodies with hard spiral-shaped shells. A snail has only one foot, which it uses to hold tightly to rocks so that it isn't swept out to sea. There are thousands of different kinds of snails. Some species are no larger than the head of a pin; others are big enough to feed on oysters and clams. The snail drills a hole through the other animal's shell. It then inserts a long feeding tube through the hole to reach the meat inside.

The starfish, or sea star, uses its five legs to move about. Each leg has rows of tiny tube feet with suckers at the tips. These suckers allow the starfish to cling to rocks or **driftwood** during wave surges. Starfish are not really fish at all. They belong to a group of creatures called *echinoderms.* Some other echinoderms are sand dollars and **sea urchins.**

Mudskippers can use their front fins to move across mudflats when the tide is out.

Mud Flats

In the tropics, the ocean tide often washes up on mud flats or mangrove swamps. Mangroves are short trees with many stilt roots. They grow in mud and saltwater along ocean shores. The stilt roots collect mud, so mangrove swamps and mud flats are often found together.

One of the strangest creatures found in these muddy tropical coastlines is the mudskipper. These unusual fish actually spend more time hopping than swimming. They use their front fins to "walk" or skip across the mud. They can even climb trees!

Mudskippers can breathe on land because there is water trapped in their gills. They do need to stay wet, however, so they need to stay near the water. Mudskippers are usually only two to four inches long, though some varieties of mudskipper grow to twelve inches in length.

Tide Pools

Life on the beach is ruled by the tides. When the tide goes out, pools of water are often left behind. Unlike the parts of the beach that are left high and dry, life goes on as usual in these pools. Because of this, tide pools offer us a closer look at what life is like in the ocean.

In a tide pool, you might see a hermit crab. Hermit crabs do not have their own shells. They live in shells that were left behind by other animals. If you have a pet hermit crab, it is important to leave an extra, larger shell in the tank with the crab. You can use **tweezers** to place the new shell near the crab. When a hermit crab outgrows its shell, it must quickly find a larger shell in which to live.

Starfish also can be found in tide pools. The starfish uses the suckers on its tube feet to grab and force open the shells of oysters. The starfish then pushes its stomach out of its body through its mouth. Chemicals in the stomach digest the oyster outside of the starfish's body.

Tide pool

Sea anemones cling to rocks in the tide pool. With their delicate colors, they look like beautiful flower blossoms in the water. But they are not flowers; they are animals. Sea anemones are not mild-mannered—their soft tentacles can sting. It would be a mistake for most creatures to view anemones as soft **hammocks** on which to rest. Anemones wave their tentacles to catch fish that might swim by them. A sea anemone will pull in its tentacles when the tide goes out to keep itself from drying out. But in a tide pool, the tentacles wave in the water.

Sea urchins are also beautiful to look at but dangerous to touch. They look like brightly colored pin cushions. Sharp spikes cover the sea urchin's soft body. These spikes discourage other creatures from wanting to make a meal of the sea urchin. The sea urchin's mouth is on its underside. The underside also has five sharp teeth that are strong enough to anchor the sea urchin to rock and coral.

A sea anemone looks more like a flower than an animal.

Fiddler crab

Salt Marshes

A salt marsh is an area that is affected by tides but is protected from big ocean waves and storms. A strip of land or some other feature keeps things calm in the salt marsh, while still allowing saltwater to flow in and out.

Salt marshes often occur near the mouths of rivers. The rivers deposit dirt, and thick mats of marsh grass grow in this dirt. Only plants that can tolerate salt will grow in these marshes. In the water and among the grasses of the salt marsh, oysters, shrimps, crabs, and flatfish make their homes.

Fiddler crabs scamper about the marshes at low tide looking for food. When the water rushes in at high tide, the crabs go back to their holes. These crabs are small—usually only an inch across. The fiddler is named for the male's huge single claw, which looks like the crab is holding a violin. Males wave their large claws to show off for female crabs.

Crabs

Fiddler crabs and hermit crabs are only two of the thousands of different kinds of crabs that live along the world's coastlines. There are king crabs, spider crabs, snow crabs, red crabs, kelp crabs, and more. Crabs come in many sizes and colors. Some crabs measure less than an inch across, but a Tasmanian crab can weigh 20 pounds and have a shell that is 18 inches across.

Crabs have no skeletons inside. It is their shells that give them shape and make it possible for them to walk. Crabs generally move with a quick, sideways motion, rather than walking straight ahead. And crabs have claws, or pincers, that they can use for feeding, fighting, or holding on.

One very interesting crab is the ghost crab. These crabs can seem to appear from nowhere. Their sand-colored shells and quick movements can make them seem to disappear before your eyes. Ghost crabs spend their days digging in the sand to make burrows. At night, they come out of their burrows to feed on clams, insects, plants, and other crabs.

The animal known as a horseshoe crab is not a crab at all. It is related to spiders and scorpions. Beneath its shell is a body that actually has more legs than a spider has. The horseshoe crab can grow as big as twenty inches in length, so it is also much larger than a spider! This strange creature burrows in the sand to find food and shelter. While the horseshoe crab is basically harmless, you still don't want to step on that sharp tail spine.

Stingray

Life on the Bottom

The mud and sand under shallow waters are also home to a great variety of marine life.

Clams and oysters live in the mud. These creatures have two hard shells that they can open and close. A clam has a muscular foot for digging in the mud. This foot helps the clam bury itself in the sand or mud. Clams have two tiny tubes, called siphons, for breathing under the mud. The siphons are pushed up to the water. One tube inhales water. The clam's gills remove the oxygen from the seawater. Then the seawater is exhaled through the other tube.

Oysters live together in beds. These beds are large groups of oysters piled on top of each other. Sometimes, a grain of sand becomes stuck inside an oyster's shell. The sand is very irritating to the oyster. The oyster covers the grain with layers of the same material it used to make its shell. Over time, a pearl is formed.

The stingray lives in warm, shallow waters and dines on the clams and oysters there. The stingray is a flat fish with a long tail that it can use like a whip. On the tail are sharp, poisonous spines. Many swimmers have **lamented** their carelessness at entering the water; stepping on a stingray can lead to a horribly painful sting.

Oysters

Coral Reefs

Coral reefs are beautiful and amazing formations. Reefs are found in shallow, tropical waters worldwide, close to the shores of many continents and islands. The water must be clear and warm for the reef to thrive. Coral reefs also need plenty of sunlight. The **algae** and other sea plants living on the reef need the sun's energy to make food.

A coral reef is home to creatures such as fish, worms, clams, turtles, and eels. Some of Earth's most colorful animals live on reefs. The reef may look like a pile of rocks to you, but it is actually built from the skeletons of millions of tiny coral animals.

There are more than 2,000 different types of coral. The corals known as stony corals are hard. There are also many soft corals. Corals can be pink, green, orange, red, or violet, but most are yellow-brown. Corals get their color from algae that live in the coral.

The body of the coral animal is called a polyp. The polyp is hollow and shaped like a cylinder. The base of the coral polyp is anchored to rock or to other corals. Tiny tentacles for gathering food surround the mouth of the coral polyp. Water currents carry food to the waiting tentacles of the coral polyp.

A large, red-brown sea fan is home to many other sea creatures.

The polyps of stony corals remove minerals from seawater to build outer skeletons. As polyps die, the skeletons are left behind, forming the reef. Most coral reefs grow less than one-fourth of an inch per year. It takes thousands of years for a large reef to be built up.

Soft corals are the most brightly colored corals. They grow in colonies that form structures that look like branches, fingers, or shelves. Soft corals do not build the reef, but they protect reefs during storms.

Sea fans are corals that are common in shallow waters. Their branching forms can grow to lengths of ten feet.

Kinds of Coral Reefs

There are three major types of coral reefs: fringing reefs, barrier reefs, and atolls. Fringing reefs are young reefs, and they are smaller in size. They are found close to the shoreline.

Barrier reefs are found farther from shore than fringing reefs. These reefs form a barrier between a lagoon and the open sea. A lagoon is a body of water separated from the sea. Australia's Great Barrier Reef is the largest group of coral reefs in the world. This barrier reef is about 1,250 miles long.

An atoll is a ring-shaped reef that forms when an old volcano sinks back into the sea. The reef grows on the volcano's rim. The coral builds upward and can even break the water's surface and become an island. There are islands in the South Pacific that have formed from atolls.

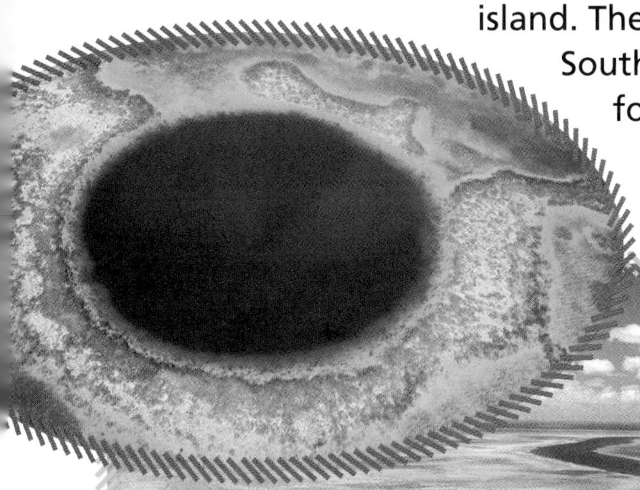

Belize's Lighthouse Reef Atoll

Australia's Great Barrier Reef

Coral Reef Fish

Corals aren't the only beautifully colored creatures living on the reef. Many of the fish that live near a coral reef come in a dazzling array of colors. For some fish, their bright colors are camouflage that allows them to blend in with the colors of the reef and avoid predators.

Sometimes, a fish's pattern or bright color serves as a warning to its predators. The lionfish is one of the most distinctive reef fish. Its unusual pattern and sharp spines alert other fish that it is poisonous.

Some fish can change their color. For example, the blue tang is bright blue during the day. At night, white bars appear on its body.

Lionfish

Blue tang

Sometimes, reef fish use camouflage to lure and trap their prey. The trumpetfish can change its color to match its background. Trumpetfish are long and skinny. They can make certain parts of their bodies different colors. If the trumpetfish wants to hunt a small yellow fish, it can turn only its head yellow. The rest of the fish's body would match the background. The prey would think it was swimming past a small yellow fish like itself.

Fish living near coral reefs have other tricks with which to fool their predators and save themselves from becoming another creature's dinner. Many small fish swim together in large schools or groups. Because they form a larger mass, a school of fish can trick a potential adversary into thinking they are one huge fish. The pufferfish also uses the idea of a larger size to scare away attackers. When threatened, the pufferfish blows itself up like a balloon. As a much larger fish, it might scare away a hungry predator.

Eels

Eels are long fish that look a lot like snakes. The moray eel has strong jaws and sharp teeth. Some moray eels can grow to ten feet long. During the day, moray eels stay **concealed** in holes in the reef. With a snap of their jaws, moray eels deal **sternly** with anyone invading their space. At night, the moray eel leaves its home to search for crabs or perhaps a small octopus.

Octopus

Like the moray eel, the octopus does not have the bright colors of tropical fish. An octopus has speed, cunning, and the ability to change colors.

An octopus has a soft round body, large eyes, and eight long arms. It can use the suckers on its arms to move around the ocean floor or it can squirt water out of a tube and zoom through the water. If an octopus looses an arm, it can grow a new one!

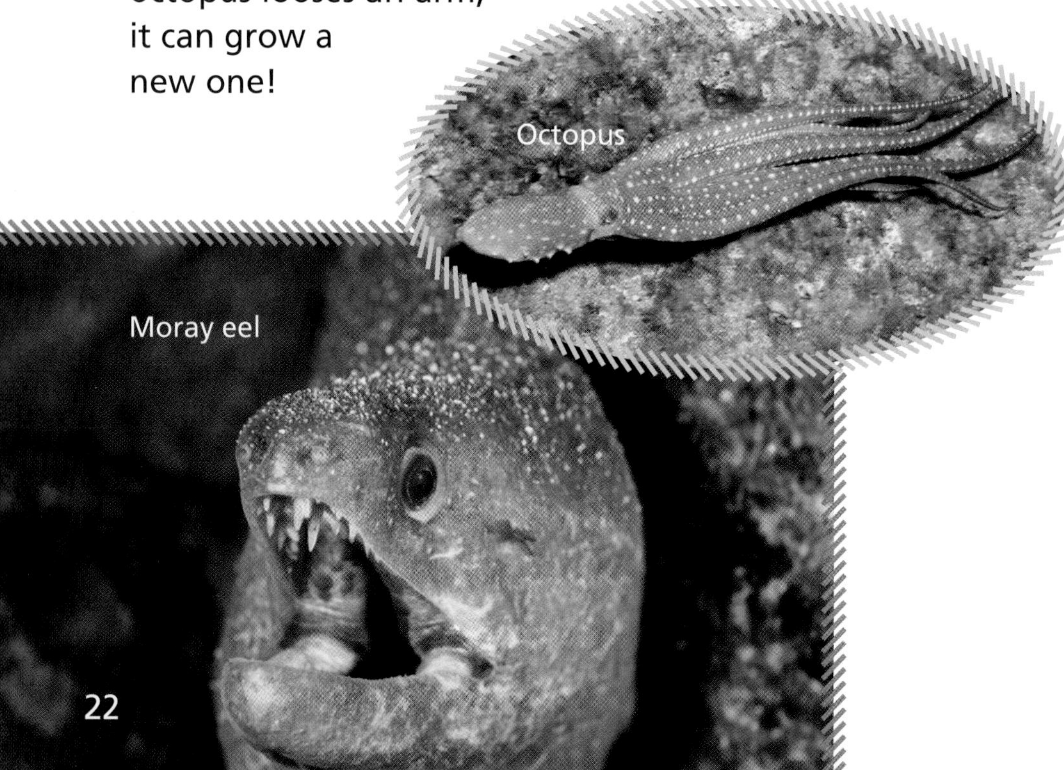

Octopus

Moray eel

Sponges

Sponges are sea animals. Most live in warm tropical waters. Some sponges are as small as a peanut. Other sponges can grow as large as a small car. Sponges come in different shapes. Some look like giant barrels or flower vases. Sponges can be bright yellow, orange, purple, gray, or brown.

Sponges attach themselves to rocks, plants, or coral reefs. Water flowing through a sponge brings in tiny animals and plant matter.

There are thousands more creatures living in the oceans and along the shores. These regions are rich with life, sometimes beautiful and sometimes strange. Scientists learn more about marine life every day.

Glossary

algae *n.* plant or plantlike organisms that live in oceans, lakes, rivers, or ponds. A single organism is called an alga.

concealed *v.* hidden from view.

driftwood *n.* wood that drifts or floats in water or that has been washed up onshore.

hammocks *n.* hanging beds made of fabric and suspended by ropes on either side.

lamented *v.* to have shown sorrow or regret.

sea urchins *n.* small, round sea animals with spiny shells.

sternly *adv.* Harshly or severely.

tweezers *n.* a metal instrument with two pieces joined at one end for picking up small objects.